Securing the Corporate Fortress: A Guide to Managing Different Security Departments in a Large Corporation

Table Of Contents

Chapter 1: Introduction to Corporate Security Departments	4
The Role of Security Departments in a Large Corporation	4
Overview of Different Security Departments	5
Importance of Managing Security Departments Effectively	6
Chapter 2: Physical Security Department	8
Securing the Physical Premises of the Corporation	8
Access Control Systems	9
Surveillance Technologies	10
Security Patrols and Guards	12
Chapter 3: Cybersecurity Department	13
Protecting Digital Assets	13
Cyber Threats and Risks	14
Preventing Hacking and Data Breaches	16
Chapter 4: Information Security Department	17
Ensuring Information Confidentiality	17
Maintaining Information Integrity	18
Ensuring Information Availability	20
Chapter 5: Risk Management Department	21
Identifying Security Risks	21
Assessing Risk Levels	22
Developing Risk Mitigation Strategies	23
Chapter 6: Compliance Department	25

Securing the Corporate Fortress: A Guide to Managing Different Security Departments in a Large Corporation

    Security Regulations and Standards   25

    Ensuring Compliance   26

    Consequences of Non-Compliance   27

Chapter 7: Fraud Prevention Department   **28**

    Detecting Fraudulent Activities   28

    Preventing Financial Fraud   29

    Preventing Identity Theft   31

Chapter 8: Emergency Response Department   **32**

    Developing Emergency Response Plans   32

    Implementing Response Strategies   33

    Training Employees for Emergencies   35

Chapter 9: Employee Security Awareness Department   **36**

    Educating Employees on Security Best Practices   36

    Promoting a Security-Conscious Culture   38

    Conducting Security Awareness Training   39

Chapter 10: Supply Chain Security Department   **40**

    Managing Security Risks in the Supply Chain   41

    Preventing Counterfeit Goods   42

    Mitigating Supplier Fraud   43

Chapter 11: Executive Protection Department   **44**

    Providing Security Services for Executives   44

    Personal Security Details   45

    Secure Transportation for High-Profile Executives   46

Chapter 12: Conclusion and Future Trends in Corporate Security Management   **47**

Securing the Corporate Fortress: A Guide to Managing Different Security Departments in a Large Corporation

Recap of Managing Different Security Departments	47
Emerging Trends in Corporate Security	49
Recommendations for Improving Corporate Security Practices	50

Chapter 1: Introduction to Corporate Security Departments

The Role of Security Departments in a Large Corporation

In a large corporation, the role of security departments is crucial in ensuring the safety and protection of the organization's assets, employees, and reputation. Each security department plays a unique and essential role in safeguarding the corporation from various threats and risks. From physical security to cybersecurity, risk management to compliance, each department contributes to the overall security posture of the corporation.

The Physical Security Department is responsible for securing the physical premises of the corporation, including access control, surveillance, and security patrols. This department ensures that only authorized personnel have access to the premises and that potential security threats are promptly identified and addressed. By implementing robust security measures, the Physical Security Department helps to deter unauthorized access and protect the corporation's physical assets.

The Cybersecurity Department manages the organization's digital assets and protects them from cyber threats, such as hacking and data breaches. With the increasing reliance on technology and digital systems, cybersecurity has become a critical aspect of corporate security. The Cybersecurity Department implements advanced security measures to safeguard the corporation's data and network infrastructure from cyberattacks, ensuring the confidentiality, integrity, and availability of digital assets.

The Information Security Department is responsible for ensuring the confidentiality, integrity, and availability of the corporation's information assets. This department implements policies and procedures to protect sensitive information from unauthorized access or disclosure. By employing encryption, access controls, and other security measures, the Information Security Department helps to safeguard the corporation's intellectual property, customer data, and other sensitive information.

Securing the Corporate Fortress: A Guide to Managing Different Security Departments in a Large Corporation

The Risk Management Department identifies and assesses potential security risks to the corporation and develops strategies to mitigate them. By conducting risk assessments and implementing risk mitigation measures, this department helps the corporation to proactively address security threats and vulnerabilities. By addressing security risks in a systematic and strategic manner, the Risk Management Department helps to enhance the overall security posture of the corporation.

The Compliance Department ensures that the corporation complies with relevant security regulations and industry standards. By staying abreast of the latest security regulations and requirements, this department helps the corporation to avoid costly fines and penalties. By implementing compliance programs and monitoring adherence to security standards, the Compliance Department helps to maintain the corporation's reputation and credibility in the marketplace.

Overview of Different Security Departments

The security of a large corporation is a multifaceted endeavor that requires the coordination of various specialized departments. In this subchapter, we will provide an overview of the different security departments commonly found in large corporations and the key responsibilities of each department. By understanding the roles and functions of these departments, security professionals can effectively manage the security operations of their organization.

One of the fundamental security departments in a large corporation is the Physical Security Department. This department is responsible for securing the physical premises of the corporation, including access control, surveillance, and security patrols. Physical security measures such as security cameras, alarm systems, and security guards are typically managed by this department to ensure the safety and security of the corporation's facilities and assets.

Securing the Corporate Fortress: A Guide to Managing Different Security Departments in a Large Corporation

In today's digital age, the Cybersecurity Department plays a critical role in protecting the organization's digital assets from cyber threats. This department is tasked with managing the organization's information technology infrastructure, implementing security measures to prevent hacking and data breaches, and responding to cyber incidents. With the increasing frequency and sophistication of cyber attacks, the Cybersecurity Department is essential for safeguarding the corporation's sensitive information and maintaining the trust of stakeholders.

The Information Security Department is another crucial component of the security infrastructure in a large corporation. This department is responsible for ensuring the confidentiality, integrity, and availability of the corporation's information assets. Information security professionals are tasked with implementing security controls, conducting risk assessments, and developing security policies and procedures to protect the organization's data from unauthorized access or disclosure.

In addition to protecting against external threats, the Risk Management Department focuses on identifying and assessing potential security risks to the corporation and developing strategies to mitigate them. By conducting risk assessments, analyzing vulnerabilities, and implementing risk mitigation measures, the Risk Management Department helps the organization proactively manage security risks and protect against potential threats to the business.

Compliance with security regulations and industry standards is a top priority for large corporations, and the Compliance Department is responsible for ensuring that the organization meets these requirements. This department monitors regulatory changes, conducts audits, and implements security controls to ensure that the corporation complies with relevant security regulations and industry best practices. By maintaining compliance with security standards, the Compliance Department helps the organization avoid legal and financial consequences associated with security breaches.

Importance of Managing Security Departments Effectively

Securing the Corporate Fortress: A Guide to Managing Different Security Departments in a Large Corporation

In today's corporate landscape, managing security departments effectively is crucial to ensure the protection of a large corporation's assets and reputation. The various security departments within a corporation play a vital role in safeguarding the physical premises, digital assets, information, and employees from potential security threats. Therefore, it is essential for professionals in charge of managing these departments to understand the importance of their roles and responsibilities.

One of the key reasons why managing security departments effectively is important is to maintain the overall security posture of the corporation. By ensuring that each security department is operating efficiently and effectively, professionals can help prevent security breaches, data leaks, and other potential threats that could harm the corporation. This proactive approach to security management can help protect the corporation's assets and reputation, as well as avoid costly security incidents.

Another important aspect of managing security departments effectively is to ensure compliance with relevant security regulations and industry standards. Professionals must stay abreast of the ever-evolving security landscape and ensure that their security departments are up to date with the latest security protocols and best practices. By doing so, they can help mitigate security risks and prevent potential legal repercussions for non-compliance.

Additionally, managing security departments effectively can help improve the overall security culture within the corporation. By promoting security awareness and education among employees, professionals can foster a security-conscious environment where everyone plays a role in protecting the corporation's assets. This can help create a strong security culture that is resilient against potential security threats and breaches.

Overall, the effective management of different security departments within a large corporation is essential for safeguarding the organization's assets and reputation. By understanding the importance of their roles and responsibilities, professionals can help ensure that each security department operates efficiently and effectively to protect the corporation from potential security threats. This proactive approach to security management can help mitigate risks, ensure compliance, and foster a security-conscious culture within the corporation.

Chapter 2: Physical Security Department

Securing the Physical Premises of the Corporation

Securing the physical premises of a corporation is a critical aspect of overall security management. The Physical Security Department plays a key role in ensuring that the company's facilities are protected from unauthorized access, theft, vandalism, and other threats. This department is responsible for implementing access control measures, such as key card systems, security guards, and perimeter fencing, to keep intruders out and protect employees and assets within the premises.

Surveillance is another important component of physical security. By installing cameras and monitoring systems, the Physical Security Department can keep a watchful eye on the premises and quickly respond to any suspicious activity. Security patrols are also essential for maintaining a visible presence and deterring potential threats. Regular patrols of the facility, both inside and out, can help identify security vulnerabilities and prevent incidents before they occur.

In addition to preventing physical threats, the Physical Security Department must also be prepared to respond to emergencies. This includes developing and practicing evacuation plans, conducting regular drills, and coordinating with local law enforcement and emergency services. By having a well-trained and responsive team in place, the department can minimize the impact of security incidents and protect the safety of employees and visitors.

Securing the Corporate Fortress: A Guide to Managing Different Security Departments in a Large Corporation

Collaboration with other security departments is crucial for a comprehensive security strategy. The Physical Security Department should work closely with the Cybersecurity Department to ensure that digital assets are protected from physical breaches, such as theft of computers or servers. Likewise, coordination with the Risk Management Department can help identify potential vulnerabilities in the physical premises and develop strategies to mitigate them.

Overall, securing the physical premises of a corporation requires a multi-faceted approach that combines access control, surveillance, security patrols, emergency response planning, and collaboration with other security departments. By taking a proactive and holistic approach to physical security, organizations can create a safe and secure environment for employees, visitors, and assets.

Access Control Systems

Access control systems play a critical role in securing the physical premises of a large corporation. These systems are designed to regulate who has access to different areas of the building, ensuring that only authorized personnel can enter sensitive areas. Access control systems can include keycard readers, biometric scanners, and PIN pads, among other technologies. By implementing access control systems, the Physical Security Department can effectively manage and monitor access to the corporation's facilities.

In addition to controlling physical access, access control systems can also be integrated with surveillance systems to enhance overall security measures. By linking access control data with video footage, security personnel can track and investigate any unauthorized access attempts. This integration allows for a more comprehensive approach to security, ensuring that any breaches are quickly detected and addressed. The Physical Security Department can use this information to improve security protocols and prevent future incidents.

The Cybersecurity Department also relies on access control systems to protect the organization's digital assets. By implementing strong authentication measures and restricting access to sensitive information, the Cybersecurity Department can prevent unauthorized users from compromising the corporation's data. Access control systems can help to limit the risk of cyber threats, such as hacking and data breaches, by ensuring that only authorized individuals can access critical systems and information.

The Information Security Department plays a crucial role in managing access control systems to safeguard the confidentiality, integrity, and availability of the corporation's information assets. By implementing robust access control policies and procedures, the Information Security Department can prevent unauthorized access to sensitive data. Access control systems can help to enforce security measures, such as encryption and multi-factor authentication, to protect the corporation's information assets from cyber threats.

Overall, access control systems are a vital component of the security infrastructure within a large corporation. By effectively managing access control systems, security departments can enhance physical security measures, protect digital assets, and ensure the confidentiality of information assets. By implementing access control systems in conjunction with other security measures, security professionals can create a comprehensive security framework to protect the corporation from a wide range of security threats.

Surveillance Technologies

Surveillance technologies play a crucial role in the overall security strategy of a large corporation. The Physical Security Department utilizes surveillance technologies to monitor and protect the physical premises of the corporation. This includes the use of CCTV cameras, access control systems, and security patrols to deter unauthorized access and detect suspicious activities. By deploying these surveillance technologies effectively, the Physical Security Department can enhance the safety and security of the corporation's employees, assets, and facilities.

Securing the Corporate Fortress: A Guide to Managing Different Security Departments in a Large Corporation

In the realm of cybersecurity, surveillance technologies are essential for monitoring and detecting potential cyber threats. The Cybersecurity Department relies on tools such as intrusion detection systems, network monitoring software, and security cameras to safeguard the organization's digital assets from hackers, malware, and other cyber threats. By continuously monitoring the organization's networks and systems, the Cybersecurity Department can identify and respond to security incidents in a timely manner, minimizing the impact of cyber attacks and data breaches.

Similarly, the Information Security Department leverages surveillance technologies to protect the confidentiality, integrity, and availability of the corporation's information assets. Through the use of data loss prevention tools, encryption technologies, and security monitoring systems, the Information Security Department can detect unauthorized access to sensitive information and prevent data breaches. By implementing robust surveillance measures, the Information Security Department can safeguard the corporation's valuable data and maintain the trust of customers, partners, and stakeholders.

In the realm of risk management, surveillance technologies play a critical role in identifying and assessing potential security risks to the corporation. The Risk Management Department utilizes surveillance tools such as threat intelligence platforms, security analytics software, and monitoring devices to track and analyze security threats and vulnerabilities. By proactively monitoring and assessing security risks, the Risk Management Department can develop effective strategies to mitigate potential threats and protect the corporation from harm.

Overall, surveillance technologies are indispensable tools for managing security departments in a large corporation. Whether it's monitoring physical premises, detecting cyber threats, protecting information assets, assessing security risks, or ensuring compliance with regulations, surveillance technologies play a vital role in safeguarding the corporation's people, assets, and reputation. By leveraging surveillance technologies effectively, security professionals can enhance the overall security posture of the corporation and mitigate potential risks and threats effectively.

Security Patrols and Guards

Security patrols and guards play a crucial role in maintaining the physical security of a large corporation. The Physical Security Department is responsible for securing the premises of the corporation, which includes implementing access control measures, conducting surveillance, and deploying security patrols. These security measures are essential for preventing unauthorized access to the premises, deterring criminal activity, and ensuring the safety of employees and assets.

Security patrols are often conducted by trained security guards who patrol the premises on foot, in vehicles, or using surveillance cameras. These patrols help to monitor the premises for any suspicious activity, respond to security incidents in a timely manner, and provide a visible deterrent to potential intruders. Security guards are also responsible for enforcing security policies, conducting security checks, and assisting with emergency response procedures.

In addition to physical security measures, the Cybersecurity Department plays a critical role in protecting the organization's digital assets from cyber threats. These threats include hacking, malware, ransomware, and data breaches, which can have devastating consequences for a corporation. The Cybersecurity Department works to identify vulnerabilities in the organization's network, systems, and applications, implement security controls to mitigate these risks, and respond to cyber incidents effectively.

The Information Security Department is tasked with ensuring the confidentiality, integrity, and availability of the corporation's information assets. This includes sensitive data, intellectual property, and proprietary information that must be protected from unauthorized access, disclosure, or modification. Information security controls, such as encryption, access controls, and data loss prevention measures, are implemented to safeguard the organization's information assets from internal and external threats.

Overall, security patrols and guards are an essential component of a comprehensive security program for a large corporation. By working in conjunction with other security departments, such as Cybersecurity, Information Security, and Risk Management, security patrols and guards help to protect the organization from physical and digital threats, mitigate security risks, and ensure the safety and security of employees, assets, and information. Effective management of security patrols and guards is essential for maintaining a strong security posture and safeguarding the corporate fortress.

Chapter 3: Cybersecurity Department

Protecting Digital Assets

Protecting digital assets is a critical aspect of managing security departments in a large corporation. The Cybersecurity Department plays a key role in this area, as it is responsible for managing the organization's digital assets and protecting them from cyber threats. This includes safeguarding sensitive data, preventing unauthorized access, and defending against hacking and data breaches. To effectively protect digital assets, the Cybersecurity Department must stay abreast of the latest cyber threats and security trends, implement robust security measures, and continuously monitor and assess the security posture of the organization's digital infrastructure.

In addition to the Cybersecurity Department, the Information Security Department also plays a crucial role in protecting digital assets. This department is responsible for ensuring the confidentiality, integrity, and availability of the corporation's information assets. This includes implementing access controls, encryption technologies, and security policies to safeguard sensitive information from unauthorized access or disclosure. The Information Security Department must also conduct regular security assessments and audits to identify vulnerabilities and weaknesses in the organization's information systems and take proactive measures to address them.

Furthermore, the Risk Management Department plays a vital role in protecting digital assets by identifying and assessing potential security risks to the corporation. This department works closely with the Cybersecurity and Information Security Departments to develop strategies to mitigate security risks and enhance the overall security posture of the organization. By conducting risk assessments, implementing risk mitigation measures, and monitoring security controls, the Risk Management Department helps to safeguard the corporation's digital assets from potential threats and vulnerabilities.

Compliance with relevant security regulations and industry standards is also essential for protecting digital assets. The Compliance Department ensures that the corporation adheres to legal and regulatory requirements related to cybersecurity and information security. By staying compliant with security regulations, the organization can avoid costly fines and penalties, as well as reputational damage resulting from security breaches or non-compliance. The Compliance Department works closely with the Cybersecurity and Information Security Departments to develop and implement security policies and procedures that align with regulatory requirements and industry best practices.

In conclusion, protecting digital assets requires a multi-faceted approach that involves collaboration among different security departments within a large corporation. By leveraging the expertise of the Cybersecurity, Information Security, Risk Management, and Compliance Departments, organizations can effectively safeguard their digital assets from cyber threats, security risks, and regulatory compliance issues. By implementing robust security measures, conducting regular security assessments, and staying compliant with relevant security regulations, corporations can create a strong security posture that protects their digital assets and minimizes the risk of security incidents.

Cyber Threats and Risks

Securing the Corporate Fortress: A Guide to Managing Different Security Departments in a Large Corporation

Cyber threats and risks are a major concern for all organizations, including large corporations with multiple security departments. The Cybersecurity Department plays a crucial role in managing the organization's digital assets and protecting them from various cyber threats, such as hacking and data breaches. With the increasing reliance on technology and the internet for conducting business operations, the risk of cyber attacks has never been higher. It is imperative for professionals in this department to stay ahead of the latest threats and continuously update their security measures to safeguard the organization's valuable information.

In today's digital age, cyber threats are constantly evolving and becoming more sophisticated. Hackers are always on the lookout for vulnerabilities in the organization's network and systems to exploit for their malicious purposes. The Cybersecurity Department must be vigilant in monitoring for any suspicious activities and proactively respond to potential threats before they escalate into major security breaches. By implementing robust security protocols, regular security audits, and employee training programs, professionals in this department can effectively mitigate the risks posed by cyber threats.

One of the biggest challenges faced by the Cybersecurity Department is the rapid pace at which new technologies are being adopted within the organization. While these technologies bring numerous benefits and efficiencies, they also introduce new vulnerabilities that cyber attackers can exploit. Professionals in this department must work closely with other security departments, such as the Information Security Department and the Risk Management Department, to identify potential security risks associated with new technologies and develop strategies to mitigate them effectively.

In addition to external cyber threats, organizations must also be mindful of internal risks posed by employees who may inadvertently compromise the organization's security. The Employee Security Awareness Department plays a crucial role in educating employees about security best practices and promoting a security-conscious culture within the organization. By fostering a culture of security awareness and accountability among employees, professionals in this department can significantly reduce the risk of insider threats and prevent security incidents caused by human error.

Overall, managing cyber threats and risks requires a comprehensive and integrated approach involving multiple security departments working together towards a common goal of protecting the organization's digital assets. By staying proactive, adapting to the latest security trends, and fostering a culture of security awareness throughout the organization, professionals can effectively safeguard the corporate fortress against cyber threats and ensure the continuity of business operations.

Preventing Hacking and Data Breaches

Preventing hacking and data breaches is a critical aspect of managing the cybersecurity department within a large corporation. In today's digital age, where cyber threats are constantly evolving, it is essential for professionals in charge of cybersecurity to stay ahead of potential attacks and protect the organization's digital assets. This subchapter will discuss key strategies for preventing hacking and data breaches, as well as best practices for managing the cybersecurity department effectively.

One of the first steps in preventing hacking and data breaches is to conduct regular security assessments and audits of the organization's digital infrastructure. This includes identifying potential vulnerabilities in the network, applications, and systems, and taking proactive measures to address them before they can be exploited by hackers. By staying vigilant and continuously monitoring for potential threats, cybersecurity professionals can reduce the risk of data breaches and unauthorized access to sensitive information.

Another important aspect of preventing hacking and data breaches is implementing robust access control measures. This includes restricting access to sensitive data and systems to only authorized personnel, implementing strong password policies, and using multi-factor authentication to verify the identity of users. By limiting access to critical assets and implementing strict authentication measures, cybersecurity professionals can reduce the likelihood of unauthorized access and data breaches.

Training employees on security best practices is also essential for preventing hacking and data breaches. Many data breaches occur due to human error, such as clicking on phishing emails or using weak passwords. By educating employees on how to recognize and respond to potential security threats, cybersecurity professionals can help create a security-conscious culture within the organization and reduce the risk of data breaches caused by employee negligence.

In addition to these proactive measures, cybersecurity professionals should also have a robust incident response plan in place to quickly detect, respond to, and recover from security incidents. This includes having protocols in place for containing and mitigating the impact of a data breach, as well as communicating effectively with stakeholders and regulatory authorities. By having a well-defined incident response plan, cybersecurity professionals can minimize the damage caused by a security incident and protect the organization's reputation.

Overall, preventing hacking and data breaches requires a combination of proactive measures, including conducting regular security assessments, implementing access control measures, training employees on security best practices, and having a robust incident response plan. By following these best practices and staying vigilant, cybersecurity professionals can help secure the corporate fortress and protect the organization's digital assets from cyber threats.

Chapter 4: Information Security Department

Ensuring Information Confidentiality

Ensuring Information Confidentiality is a critical aspect of managing a large corporation's security departments. The Information Security Department plays a key role in safeguarding the confidentiality, integrity, and availability of the organization's information assets. This includes sensitive data such as customer information, intellectual property, and financial records. To effectively protect this valuable information, it is essential to implement robust security measures and protocols.

One of the first steps in ensuring information confidentiality is to conduct a comprehensive risk assessment. This involves identifying potential security threats and vulnerabilities that could compromise the confidentiality of the corporation's information assets. By understanding these risks, security professionals can develop targeted strategies to mitigate them and minimize the likelihood of a security breach.

Access control is another crucial aspect of ensuring information confidentiality. By limiting access to sensitive information to authorized personnel only, organizations can reduce the risk of unauthorized disclosure or data theft. This can be achieved through the use of authentication mechanisms such as passwords, biometric scanners, and access control systems that restrict entry to designated areas.

Encryption is a powerful tool for protecting the confidentiality of information. By encrypting data both at rest and in transit, organizations can ensure that even if it is intercepted by unauthorized parties, it remains unreadable and secure. Implementing encryption protocols and technologies across all communication channels and storage systems is essential for safeguarding sensitive information from prying eyes.

Regular security training and awareness programs are also vital for ensuring information confidentiality. Employees are often the weakest link in an organization's security posture, as they may inadvertently expose sensitive information through careless actions or lack of awareness. By educating staff about security best practices, the risks of data breaches, and the importance of protecting confidential information, companies can empower their workforce to become proactive defenders of corporate data privacy.

Maintaining Information Integrity

Securing the Corporate Fortress: A Guide to Managing Different Security Departments in a Large Corporation

Maintaining information integrity is a crucial aspect of managing different security departments in a large corporation. The Information Security Department plays a vital role in ensuring the confidentiality, integrity, and availability of the corporation's information assets. This includes protecting sensitive data from unauthorized access, ensuring data is not tampered with or altered, and ensuring information is accessible when needed. To maintain information integrity, the Information Security Department must implement robust access controls, encryption protocols, and regular audits to monitor and protect data.

In addition to the Information Security Department, the Cybersecurity Department also plays a key role in maintaining information integrity. This department is responsible for managing the organization's digital assets and protecting them from cyber threats, such as hacking and data breaches. By implementing firewalls, intrusion detection systems, and security patches, the Cybersecurity Department helps to safeguard the corporation's information assets from malicious actors seeking to compromise data integrity. Regular security assessments and penetration testing are also essential to identify and address vulnerabilities before they can be exploited.

Collaboration between the Information Security Department and the Cybersecurity Department is essential for maintaining information integrity. By working together to identify and mitigate security risks, these departments can ensure that the corporation's information assets remain secure and protected. Regular communication and information sharing between these departments can help to proactively address potential threats and vulnerabilities, reducing the risk of data breaches and other security incidents that could compromise information integrity.

Furthermore, the Risk Management Department plays a crucial role in maintaining information integrity by identifying and assessing potential security risks to the corporation. By developing strategies to mitigate these risks, such as implementing data encryption, conducting regular security training for employees, and implementing multi-factor authentication, the Risk Management Department helps to protect the integrity of the corporation's information assets. By taking a proactive approach to risk management, this department can help to prevent security incidents that could compromise information integrity.

Overall, maintaining information integrity requires a multi-faceted approach that involves collaboration between different security departments within a large corporation. By working together to implement robust security measures, monitor for potential threats, and respond quickly to security incidents, these departments can help to ensure that the corporation's information assets remain secure and protected. By prioritizing information integrity and investing in the necessary resources and technologies, corporations can safeguard their sensitive data and maintain the trust of their stakeholders.

Ensuring Information Availability

In today's digital age, information is one of the most valuable assets of any corporation. It is crucial for organizations to ensure the availability of their information assets to support business operations and decision-making processes. The Information Security Department plays a key role in ensuring the confidentiality, integrity, and availability of the corporation's information assets. This department is responsible for implementing measures to prevent unauthorized access to information, protect data from loss or corruption, and ensure that information is available when needed.

One of the key challenges faced by the Information Security Department is ensuring the availability of information in the face of cyber threats. Cybersecurity incidents, such as hacking and data breaches, can disrupt business operations and compromise the integrity of information assets. To mitigate these risks, the Information Security Department must implement robust security measures, such as firewalls, encryption, and intrusion detection systems, to protect information assets from unauthorized access and cyber attacks.

In addition to cyber threats, the Information Security Department must also address other factors that can impact the availability of information, such as hardware failures, natural disasters, and human errors. To ensure the availability of information in the event of these incidents, the department should develop and implement disaster recovery and business continuity plans. These plans outline procedures for restoring information systems and data in the event of a disruption, ensuring that critical business functions can continue without interruption.

Furthermore, the Information Security Department should work closely with other security departments, such as the Physical Security Department and the Risk Management Department, to ensure a comprehensive approach to information security. By collaborating with these departments, the Information Security Department can identify potential risks to information availability and develop strategies to mitigate them. This collaborative approach helps to create a strong security posture that protects the corporation's information assets from a wide range of threats.

Ultimately, ensuring the availability of information is essential for the success and resilience of any corporation. By implementing robust security measures, developing disaster recovery and business continuity plans, and collaborating with other security departments, the Information Security Department can effectively protect the availability of the corporation's information assets and support business operations in the face of evolving security threats.

Chapter 5: Risk Management Department

Identifying Security Risks

In any large corporation, it is crucial to have a comprehensive understanding of the potential security risks that could threaten the organization. This involves identifying vulnerabilities in various areas, such as physical security, cybersecurity, information security, risk management, compliance, fraud prevention, emergency response, employee security awareness, supply chain security, and executive protection. By proactively identifying these risks, security departments can develop strategies to mitigate them effectively.

The Physical Security Department plays a vital role in securing the physical premises of the corporation. This includes implementing access control measures, surveillance systems, and security patrols to prevent unauthorized access and protect the organization's assets. By conducting regular security assessments and audits, the Physical Security Department can identify vulnerabilities in the physical infrastructure and address them before they are exploited by malicious actors.

Securing the Corporate Fortress: A Guide to Managing Different Security Departments in a Large Corporation

The Cybersecurity Department is responsible for managing the organization's digital assets and protecting them from cyber threats. This involves implementing robust cybersecurity measures, such as firewalls, antivirus software, and intrusion detection systems, to prevent hacking and data breaches. By conducting regular penetration testing and threat assessments, the Cybersecurity Department can identify potential vulnerabilities in the organization's IT systems and take proactive measures to secure them.

The Information Security Department is tasked with ensuring the confidentiality, integrity, and availability of the corporation's information assets. This includes implementing encryption, access controls, and data loss prevention measures to protect sensitive information from unauthorized access or disclosure. By conducting regular security audits and risk assessments, the Information Security Department can identify potential security gaps in the organization's information systems and develop strategies to mitigate them effectively.

The Risk Management Department plays a critical role in identifying and assessing potential security risks to the corporation. This involves conducting risk assessments, analyzing threat intelligence, and developing strategies to mitigate security risks. By collaborating with other security departments and stakeholders, the Risk Management Department can develop comprehensive risk management plans that address the organization's most critical security challenges.

Assessing Risk Levels

Assessing risk levels is a critical component of managing security departments within a large corporation. Each department, whether it be Physical Security, Cybersecurity, Information Security, Risk Management, Compliance, Fraud Prevention, Emergency Response, Employee Security Awareness, Supply Chain Security, or Executive Protection, must have a clear understanding of the potential risks facing the organization in order to effectively mitigate them. By assessing risk levels, security professionals can prioritize their efforts and allocate resources in a strategic manner.

In the Physical Security Department, assessing risk levels involves evaluating vulnerabilities in the corporation's physical premises, such as access control points, surveillance systems, and security patrols. By identifying weak points in the physical security infrastructure, security professionals can implement measures to strengthen security and prevent unauthorized access. Conducting regular risk assessments can help the department stay ahead of potential security threats and ensure the safety of employees and assets.

For the Cybersecurity Department, assessing risk levels means understanding the potential cyber threats facing the organization, such as hacking, malware, and data breaches. By conducting regular risk assessments, security professionals can identify vulnerabilities in the organization's digital assets and develop strategies to protect against cyber attacks. This proactive approach to risk management is essential in today's digital age, where cyber threats are constantly evolving and becoming more sophisticated.

The Information Security Department is responsible for ensuring the confidentiality, integrity, and availability of the corporation's information assets. By assessing risk levels, security professionals can identify potential weaknesses in the organization's information security practices and develop measures to protect sensitive data from unauthorized access or disclosure. Regular risk assessments are essential in maintaining the security of information assets and preventing data breaches that could have serious consequences for the organization.

In conclusion, assessing risk levels is a fundamental aspect of managing security departments within a large corporation. By understanding the potential risks facing the organization, security professionals can develop proactive strategies to mitigate security threats and protect the organization's assets. Whether it be in Physical Security, Cybersecurity, Information Security, Risk Management, Compliance, Fraud Prevention, Emergency Response, Employee Security Awareness, Supply Chain Security, or Executive Protection, assessing risk levels is essential for maintaining a secure corporate fortress.

Developing Risk Mitigation Strategies

Securing the Corporate Fortress: A Guide to Managing Different Security Departments in a Large Corporation

Developing risk mitigation strategies is a crucial aspect of managing different security departments in a large corporation. In order to effectively protect the organization from potential threats, it is essential to identify and assess potential security risks and develop strategies to mitigate them. This involves taking a proactive approach to security, rather than waiting for a security incident to occur before taking action.

One key aspect of developing risk mitigation strategies is understanding the specific vulnerabilities and threats that the organization faces. This requires collaboration between different security departments, such as the Physical Security Department, Cybersecurity Department, Information Security Department, Risk Management Department, Compliance Department, Fraud Prevention Department, Emergency Response Department, Employee Security Awareness Department, Supply Chain Security Department, and Executive Protection Department. By working together, these departments can identify potential risks and develop comprehensive strategies to address them.

Risk mitigation strategies may involve a combination of physical security measures, cybersecurity protocols, information security controls, risk assessments, compliance audits, fraud detection systems, emergency response plans, employee training programs, supply chain security measures, and executive protection services. These strategies should be tailored to the specific needs and vulnerabilities of the organization, taking into account factors such as industry regulations, business operations, geographic location, and threat landscape.

In developing risk mitigation strategies, it is important to prioritize security risks based on their potential impact on the organization. This involves conducting risk assessments to identify high-risk areas and developing strategies to mitigate these risks first. By focusing on the most critical security risks, security departments can allocate resources effectively and address vulnerabilities before they can be exploited by malicious actors.

Ultimately, developing risk mitigation strategies is an ongoing process that requires continuous monitoring, evaluation, and improvement. By staying vigilant and proactive in identifying and addressing security risks, organizations can better protect themselves from potential threats and safeguard their assets, employees, and reputation. Effective risk mitigation strategies are essential for securing the corporate fortress and maintaining a strong security posture in today's rapidly evolving threat landscape.

Chapter 6: Compliance Department

Security Regulations and Standards

Security regulations and standards play a crucial role in the operations of different security departments within a large corporation. These regulations provide a framework for ensuring the protection of the corporation's physical premises, digital assets, information assets, and overall security posture. By adhering to these regulations, security departments can effectively manage security risks, prevent fraudulent activities, and respond efficiently to security incidents.

The Physical Security Department focuses on securing the physical premises of the corporation, including access control, surveillance, and security patrols. In order to comply with security regulations and standards, this department must implement measures such as installing security cameras, access control systems, and conducting regular security patrols to prevent unauthorized access to the premises. By following these regulations, the Physical Security Department can ensure the safety and security of the corporation's employees, assets, and visitors.

The Cybersecurity Department is responsible for managing the organization's digital assets and protecting them from cyber threats, such as hacking and data breaches. To comply with security regulations and standards, this department must implement robust cybersecurity measures, such as firewalls, intrusion detection systems, and encryption techniques. By following these regulations, the Cybersecurity Department can safeguard the corporation's sensitive data and prevent cyber attacks that could compromise its operations and reputation.

Securing the Corporate Fortress: A Guide to Managing Different Security Departments in a Large Corporation

The Information Security Department is tasked with ensuring the confidentiality, integrity, and availability of the corporation's information assets. To comply with security regulations and standards, this department must implement policies and procedures to protect sensitive information from unauthorized access, disclosure, or modification. By following these regulations, the Information Security Department can mitigate the risk of data breaches and ensure the secure handling of the corporation's information assets.

The Risk Management Department plays a crucial role in identifying and assessing potential security risks to the corporation and developing strategies to mitigate them. By complying with security regulations and standards, this department can effectively manage security risks, such as natural disasters, terrorist attacks, and cyber threats. By following these regulations, the Risk Management Department can protect the corporation from potential security incidents and minimize their impact on its operations and reputation.

Ensuring Compliance

Ensuring compliance within a large corporation is essential to maintaining the security and integrity of the organization. The Compliance Department plays a crucial role in ensuring that the corporation complies with relevant security regulations and industry standards. This includes staying up-to-date on changing laws and regulations, conducting regular audits and assessments, and implementing policies and procedures to address any compliance issues that may arise.

In order to effectively ensure compliance, the Compliance Department must work closely with all other security departments within the organization. This collaboration is essential for identifying potential compliance risks and developing strategies to mitigate them. By working together, departments such as Physical Security, Cybersecurity, Information Security, Risk Management, and Fraud Prevention can ensure that the corporation is fully compliant with all relevant security regulations and standards.

One of the key responsibilities of the Compliance Department is to keep employees informed about security regulations and best practices. This includes providing training and educational programs to help employees understand their role in maintaining compliance. By promoting a security-conscious culture within the organization, the Compliance Department can help prevent security breaches and ensure that all employees are aware of their responsibilities when it comes to security compliance.

In addition to working with internal departments, the Compliance Department also plays a crucial role in managing relationships with external regulatory bodies and industry organizations. This includes staying informed about changes in security regulations and standards, as well as participating in industry forums and working groups to share best practices and stay ahead of emerging security threats.

Overall, ensuring compliance within a large corporation requires a collaborative and proactive approach. By working together with all security departments, educating employees about security best practices, and staying informed about changing regulations and standards, the Compliance Department can help the organization maintain a strong and secure corporate fortress.

Consequences of Non-Compliance

In the world of corporate security, compliance is paramount. The consequences of non-compliance can be severe and far-reaching, affecting not only the security of the corporation but also its reputation and bottom line. For professionals managing different security departments in a large corporation, understanding the repercussions of failing to comply with security regulations and industry standards is crucial.

One of the most significant consequences of non-compliance is the increased vulnerability to security threats. Without proper adherence to regulations and standards, the corporation becomes an easy target for cyber attacks, data breaches, and physical security breaches. This can result in significant financial losses, damage to the corporation's reputation, and even legal repercussions.

Furthermore, non-compliance can lead to a breakdown in trust with stakeholders, including customers, partners, and regulatory agencies. When a corporation fails to meet security requirements, stakeholders may question its ability to protect sensitive information and assets, leading to a loss of business and credibility. This can have long-lasting effects on the corporation's relationships and future opportunities.

From a legal perspective, non-compliance can result in fines, penalties, and lawsuits. Regulatory bodies have the authority to enforce compliance with security regulations, and failure to meet these requirements can result in costly consequences. In some cases, non-compliance may even lead to criminal charges for neglecting to protect sensitive information or assets.

In addition to financial and legal consequences, non-compliance can also have a negative impact on employee morale and productivity. When security measures are not properly enforced, employees may feel unsafe in their work environment, leading to increased stress and decreased job satisfaction. This can ultimately affect the corporation's overall performance and success.

Overall, the consequences of non-compliance in corporate security are significant and wide-ranging. For professionals managing different security departments in a large corporation, it is essential to prioritize compliance and ensure that all security measures are effectively implemented and maintained. By taking proactive steps to meet security regulations and industry standards, corporations can protect themselves from the damaging effects of non-compliance and maintain a strong, secure corporate fortress.

Chapter 7: Fraud Prevention Department

Detecting Fraudulent Activities

Detecting fraudulent activities is a crucial aspect of managing a comprehensive security program within a large corporation. The Fraud Prevention Department plays a key role in identifying and preventing various forms of fraud, including financial fraud and identity theft. By actively monitoring for suspicious activities and implementing effective fraud detection tools, this department helps safeguard the corporation's assets and reputation.

One of the most common forms of fraudulent activity within a corporation is financial fraud, which can result in significant financial losses and damage to the company's credibility. The Fraud Prevention Department utilizes advanced analytics and fraud detection software to identify unusual patterns or discrepancies in financial transactions. By closely monitoring financial data and conducting regular audits, this department can quickly detect and investigate any potential fraudulent activity.

In addition to financial fraud, identity theft is another prevalent threat that corporations must guard against. Cybercriminals may attempt to steal employees' personal information or compromise sensitive data through phishing scams or malware attacks. The Fraud Prevention Department works closely with the Cybersecurity Department to implement robust identity theft prevention measures, such as multi-factor authentication and encryption protocols, to protect against unauthorized access to corporate systems and data.

To enhance the effectiveness of fraud detection efforts, collaboration among different security departments is essential. The Fraud Prevention Department works in tandem with the Information Security Department to ensure that sensitive information is adequately protected and encrypted to prevent unauthorized access. Additionally, close coordination with the Risk Management Department helps identify potential vulnerabilities and develop proactive strategies to mitigate fraud risks before they escalate.

Ultimately, detecting and preventing fraudulent activities requires a proactive and multifaceted approach that involves leveraging technology, establishing strong internal controls, and fostering a culture of transparency and accountability within the organization. By investing in comprehensive fraud prevention measures and promoting a security-conscious mindset across all departments, corporations can effectively combat the ever-evolving threats posed by fraudsters and protect their valuable assets and reputation.

Preventing Financial Fraud

Securing the Corporate Fortress: A Guide to Managing Different Security Departments in a Large Corporation

Financial fraud is a serious threat to large corporations, with potentially devastating consequences for both the company and its stakeholders. In order to effectively prevent financial fraud, organizations must implement robust controls and procedures across all departments, including the Fraud Prevention Department. This specialized department is responsible for detecting and preventing fraudulent activities within the corporation, such as embezzlement, accounting fraud, and identity theft.

One of the key strategies for preventing financial fraud is to establish clear policies and procedures that govern how financial transactions are conducted within the organization. This includes implementing segregation of duties, where different individuals are responsible for initiating, approving, and reconciling financial transactions. By separating these roles, organizations can reduce the risk of fraud by ensuring that no single individual has complete control over a transaction from start to finish.

Another important aspect of preventing financial fraud is to conduct regular audits and reviews of financial processes and controls. By regularly monitoring and evaluating the effectiveness of these controls, organizations can identify potential vulnerabilities and weaknesses that could be exploited by fraudsters. Additionally, conducting thorough background checks on employees, particularly those with access to sensitive financial information, can help to prevent insider fraud.

Training and awareness programs are also essential for preventing financial fraud within a corporation. The Employee Security Awareness Department plays a key role in educating employees about the risks of fraud and promoting a security-conscious culture within the organization. By providing employees with the knowledge and tools they need to recognize and report suspicious behavior, organizations can empower their workforce to act as a first line of defense against fraud.

Collaboration between different security departments, such as the Fraud Prevention Department, Risk Management Department, and Compliance Department, is crucial for preventing financial fraud. By working together to identify and assess potential security risks, develop strategies to mitigate them, and ensure compliance with relevant regulations and industry standards, these departments can create a comprehensive and effective fraud prevention program. Ultimately, by taking a proactive and multi-faceted approach to preventing financial fraud, organizations can safeguard their assets, reputation, and bottom line.

Preventing Identity Theft

Identity theft is a serious threat in today's digital age, with cybercriminals constantly seeking to exploit vulnerabilities in order to steal personal information for fraudulent purposes. As professionals working in different security departments within a large corporation, it is crucial to understand the importance of preventing identity theft and implementing effective measures to safeguard sensitive data.

In the Physical Security Department, securing the physical premises of the corporation is a key priority. This includes implementing access control systems to restrict entry to authorized personnel only, installing surveillance cameras to monitor activity, and conducting regular security patrols to deter unauthorized individuals. By maintaining a strong physical security posture, the risk of identity theft through physical means can be significantly reduced.

The Cybersecurity Department plays a critical role in protecting the organization's digital assets from cyber threats, including identity theft. This involves implementing robust security measures such as firewalls, encryption, and intrusion detection systems to prevent unauthorized access to sensitive information. Regular security audits and penetration testing can help identify potential vulnerabilities and address them before they can be exploited by cybercriminals.

In the Information Security Department, ensuring the confidentiality, integrity, and availability of the corporation's information assets is paramount. By implementing access controls, encryption, and data loss prevention measures, sensitive information can be protected from unauthorized access or disclosure. Regular training and awareness programs can also help employees recognize and report suspicious activity that may indicate a potential identity theft attempt.

The Risk Management Department plays a crucial role in identifying and assessing potential security risks, including those related to identity theft. By conducting thorough risk assessments and developing strategies to mitigate these risks, the organization can proactively protect against identity theft incidents. Collaborating with other security departments to implement comprehensive security measures can further enhance the corporation's overall defense against identity theft.

In conclusion, preventing identity theft requires a multi-faceted approach that involves coordination between different security departments within a large corporation. By implementing physical security measures, robust cybersecurity controls, information security protocols, and risk management strategies, professionals can work together to safeguard sensitive information and protect against identity theft. By staying vigilant and proactive in addressing potential threats, organizations can mitigate the risk of falling victim to identity theft and uphold the security of their corporate fortress.

Chapter 8: Emergency Response Department

Developing Emergency Response Plans

Developing emergency response plans is a critical component of managing different security departments within a large corporation. The Emergency Response Department plays a vital role in ensuring the safety and security of employees, assets, and operations in the event of security incidents such as natural disasters, terrorist attacks, or other emergencies. By developing and implementing effective emergency response plans, organizations can minimize the impact of such incidents and protect their people and assets.

One key aspect of developing emergency response plans is conducting a thorough risk assessment to identify potential threats and vulnerabilities that could impact the corporation. This involves evaluating the likelihood and potential impact of various security incidents, as well as determining the resources and capabilities needed to respond effectively. By understanding the specific risks facing the organization, security professionals can tailor their emergency response plans to address these threats and mitigate their impact.

Another important step in developing emergency response plans is establishing clear roles and responsibilities for key personnel within the organization. This includes designating individuals to lead the response efforts, coordinating communication and information sharing, and ensuring that all employees are aware of their roles and responsibilities in the event of an emergency. By clearly defining these roles and responsibilities, organizations can ensure a coordinated and effective response to security incidents.

In addition to identifying risks and establishing roles and responsibilities, emergency response plans should also include detailed procedures for responding to different types of security incidents. This may involve creating evacuation plans, establishing communication protocols, and coordinating with external agencies such as law enforcement and emergency services. By developing detailed procedures for responding to security incidents, organizations can ensure a swift and effective response that minimizes the impact on employees and operations.

Overall, developing effective emergency response plans is essential for managing different security departments within a large corporation. By conducting risk assessments, defining roles and responsibilities, and establishing detailed procedures for responding to security incidents, organizations can enhance their preparedness and resilience in the face of emergencies. With well-developed emergency response plans in place, security professionals can effectively protect their people, assets, and operations from a wide range of security threats.

Implementing Response Strategies

Securing the Corporate Fortress: A Guide to Managing Different Security Departments in a Large Corporation

Implementing Response Strategies is a crucial aspect of managing different security departments within a large corporation. These strategies are designed to address potential security threats and incidents effectively, ensuring the safety and protection of the organization's assets, employees, and reputation. By developing and implementing response strategies, security departments can mitigate risks, respond to incidents promptly, and minimize the impact of security breaches.

In the Physical Security Department, response strategies often focus on securing the physical premises of the corporation. This includes implementing access control measures, conducting regular security patrols, and utilizing surveillance technology to monitor potential threats. In the event of a security breach or incident, the Physical Security Department must have protocols in place to respond quickly and effectively, such as emergency response plans and communication procedures.

The Cybersecurity Department is responsible for managing the organization's digital assets and protecting them from cyber threats. Response strategies in this department typically involve detecting and responding to cyber attacks, such as hacking and data breaches. This may include implementing intrusion detection systems, conducting regular security audits, and developing incident response plans to minimize the impact of cyber incidents on the organization.

The Information Security Department focuses on ensuring the confidentiality, integrity, and availability of the corporation's information assets. Response strategies in this department may include implementing encryption technologies, conducting regular security assessments, and developing data backup and recovery plans to protect sensitive information in the event of a security breach. Additionally, the Information Security Department must have incident response protocols in place to address data breaches and other security incidents promptly and effectively.

The Risk Management Department plays a critical role in identifying and assessing potential security risks to the corporation and developing strategies to mitigate them. Response strategies in this department involve conducting risk assessments, developing risk mitigation plans, and monitoring and evaluating security controls to ensure they are effective in mitigating risks. By implementing response strategies, the Risk Management Department can help the organization proactively manage security risks and respond to incidents in a timely and efficient manner.

Training Employees for Emergencies

Training employees for emergencies is a crucial aspect of ensuring the safety and security of a large corporation. In the event of a security incident or natural disaster, employees need to be prepared to respond quickly and effectively to minimize potential harm and damage. This subchapter will focus on the importance of training employees for emergencies and provide practical strategies for implementing an effective training program within the organization.

One key aspect of training employees for emergencies is to ensure that they are familiar with the corporation's emergency response procedures. This includes knowing how to evacuate the building safely, where to assemble in case of a fire or other emergency, and who to contact for assistance. It is important for employees to have easy access to this information and to regularly review and practice emergency response drills to ensure that they are prepared to respond effectively in a crisis situation.

In addition to familiarizing employees with emergency response procedures, training should also include specific instructions on how to respond to different types of emergencies. For example, employees should know how to react to a fire, medical emergency, active shooter situation, or natural disaster. This may involve providing hands-on training, such as CPR and first aid classes, as well as simulations or role-playing exercises to help employees practice their response skills in a controlled environment.

Another important aspect of training employees for emergencies is to educate them on the importance of maintaining a security-conscious mindset at all times. This includes encouraging employees to report any suspicious behavior or security concerns to the appropriate authorities, as well as emphasizing the importance of following security protocols and procedures to prevent security breaches or incidents. By promoting a culture of security awareness within the organization, employees can play an active role in protecting the corporation from potential threats.

It is also important to regularly review and update the emergency response training program to ensure that it remains relevant and effective. This may involve conducting regular drills and exercises to test employees' response skills, as well as seeking feedback from employees on ways to improve the training program. By continuously evaluating and refining the training program, the organization can better prepare employees to respond to emergencies and ensure the safety and security of the corporation.

In conclusion, training employees for emergencies is a critical component of managing security within a large corporation. By familiarizing employees with emergency response procedures, providing specific instructions on how to respond to different types of emergencies, promoting a security-conscious mindset, and regularly reviewing and updating the training program, organizations can better prepare employees to respond effectively in a crisis situation. Ultimately, investing in employee training for emergencies is an essential step in securing the corporate fortress and protecting the organization from potential threats.

Chapter 9: Employee Security Awareness Department

Educating Employees on Security Best Practices

Securing the Corporate Fortress: A Guide to Managing Different Security Departments in a Large Corporation

Educating employees on security best practices is a critical component of maintaining a secure corporate fortress. A well-informed and security-conscious workforce is the first line of defense against potential threats, both physical and digital. In this subchapter, we will explore the importance of employee security awareness and provide strategies for effectively educating employees on security best practices.

One of the primary responsibilities of the Employee Security Awareness Department is to develop and deliver training programs that educate employees on security policies, procedures, and best practices. These programs should cover a range of topics, including password security, phishing awareness, physical security protocols, and data protection guidelines. By providing employees with the knowledge and skills they need to protect themselves and the organization, the Employee Security Awareness Department plays a crucial role in building a strong security culture within the corporation.

In addition to formal training programs, the Employee Security Awareness Department should also utilize a variety of communication channels to reinforce key security messages and keep employees informed about the latest security threats and trends. This may include email newsletters, intranet articles, posters, and regular security awareness campaigns. By keeping security top of mind for employees, the department can help ensure that security remains a priority for everyone in the organization.

It is also important for the Employee Security Awareness Department to engage employees in security awareness activities and initiatives. This could involve hosting security-themed events, such as lunch and learns, workshops, or simulations of security incidents. By providing employees with hands-on opportunities to practice security best practices and learn from real-world scenarios, the department can help employees develop the skills and confidence they need to respond effectively to security threats.

Ultimately, the goal of the Employee Security Awareness Department is to create a security-conscious culture within the corporation, where employees are empowered to take an active role in protecting the organization's assets and data. By investing in employee security awareness and education, corporations can strengthen their overall security posture and reduce the risk of security incidents and breaches. In the next chapter, we will explore strategies for measuring the effectiveness of employee security awareness programs and continuously improving security education efforts within the organization.

Promoting a Security-Conscious Culture

Promoting a security-conscious culture within a large corporation is essential to ensuring the overall safety and protection of the organization's assets, employees, and reputation. This subchapter will focus on the importance of fostering a culture of security awareness and best practices across all departments, from physical security to cybersecurity and beyond.

One of the key strategies for promoting a security-conscious culture is to provide ongoing training and education for employees at all levels of the organization. This includes regular security awareness sessions, simulated security drills, and access to resources and tools that can help employees identify and respond to potential security threats. By empowering employees with the knowledge and skills they need to protect themselves and the organization, companies can significantly reduce the risk of security incidents.

In addition to training and education, it is important for leadership to set a positive example when it comes to security practices. Executives and managers should prioritize security in their decision-making processes, communicate the importance of security to all employees, and hold themselves and others accountable for following security protocols. When employees see that security is a top priority for leadership, they are more likely to take security matters seriously themselves.

Another effective way to promote a security-conscious culture is to make security a part of the organization's core values and mission statement. By embedding security principles into the company's culture, employees are more likely to view security as a fundamental aspect of their work and personal responsibilities. This can help create a sense of shared ownership and accountability for security across the entire organization.

Lastly, companies should consider implementing incentives and recognition programs to reward employees who demonstrate exemplary security practices and behaviors. By acknowledging and rewarding individuals who go above and beyond to uphold security standards, companies can reinforce the importance of security-conscious behavior and motivate others to follow suit. This can help create a positive feedback loop that encourages a culture of security awareness and vigilance throughout the organization.

In conclusion, promoting a security-conscious culture is a critical component of managing different security departments within a large corporation. By providing comprehensive training, leading by example, embedding security into core values, and incentivizing good security practices, companies can create a culture where security is everyone's responsibility. This can help mitigate security risks, protect the organization's assets, and build a strong foundation for long-term security success.

Conducting Security Awareness Training

Conducting Security Awareness Training is a crucial aspect of managing different security departments within a large corporation. This subchapter will delve into the importance of educating employees about security best practices and promoting a security-conscious culture within the organization. Security awareness training is essential in ensuring that employees are aware of potential security risks and know how to respond to security incidents effectively.

Securing the Corporate Fortress: A Guide to Managing Different Security Departments in a Large Corporation

The Employee Security Awareness Department plays a vital role in conducting security awareness training for all employees within the corporation. This department is responsible for developing and delivering training programs that cover a wide range of security topics, such as phishing scams, password security, and physical security protocols. By educating employees about these security best practices, the corporation can significantly reduce the risk of security breaches caused by human error.

When conducting security awareness training, it is essential to make the training engaging and interactive. Utilizing a variety of training methods, such as online modules, in-person workshops, and simulated phishing exercises, can help keep employees engaged and reinforce key security concepts. Additionally, incorporating real-life examples and case studies can help employees understand the potential consequences of security breaches and the importance of following security protocols.

Furthermore, it is crucial to tailor security awareness training to the specific needs of different departments within the corporation. For example, the Physical Security Department may require training on access control procedures and surveillance protocols, while the Cybersecurity Department may need training on detecting and responding to cyber threats. By customizing training programs to address the unique security requirements of each department, employees will be better equipped to protect the corporation's assets and data.

In conclusion, conducting security awareness training is essential for managing different security departments within a large corporation. By educating employees about security best practices and promoting a security-conscious culture, the corporation can significantly enhance its overall security posture. Through engaging and interactive training programs tailored to the specific needs of each department, employees will be better prepared to identify and respond to security threats, ultimately helping to secure the corporate fortress.

Chapter 10: Supply Chain Security Department

Managing Security Risks in the Supply Chain

Managing security risks in the supply chain is a critical aspect of ensuring the overall security of a large corporation. The Supply Chain Security Department is responsible for identifying and mitigating potential risks associated with the sourcing, manufacturing, and distribution of the corporation's products or services. These risks can range from counterfeit goods and supplier fraud to transportation security and regulatory compliance issues. By effectively managing these risks, the corporation can protect its reputation, financial stability, and competitive advantage.

One of the key challenges in managing supply chain security risks is the complexity and interconnected nature of modern supply chains. With multiple vendors, suppliers, and partners involved in the production and distribution process, it can be difficult to track and monitor all potential security threats. This is why it is essential for the Supply Chain Security Department to have clear policies, procedures, and controls in place to ensure the integrity and security of the supply chain.

One of the most effective ways to manage security risks in the supply chain is through regular risk assessments and audits. By conducting thorough assessments of the entire supply chain, the department can identify potential vulnerabilities and develop strategies to address them. This may include implementing stronger supplier vetting processes, conducting background checks on key partners, and establishing secure transportation protocols. By proactively addressing security risks, the corporation can reduce the likelihood of supply chain disruptions and protect its assets and reputation.

In addition to risk assessments, the Supply Chain Security Department should also establish strong relationships with key stakeholders, including vendors, suppliers, and logistics partners. By fostering open communication and collaboration, the department can build trust and transparency within the supply chain, making it easier to address security concerns and respond to potential threats. This can also help to ensure that all parties involved in the supply chain are aligned with the corporation's security objectives and compliance requirements.

Overall, managing security risks in the supply chain requires a proactive and multi-faceted approach. By implementing robust security measures, conducting regular risk assessments, and fostering strong relationships with key stakeholders, the Supply Chain Security Department can help to safeguard the corporation's assets, reputation, and competitive edge. By taking a strategic and holistic approach to supply chain security, the department can contribute to the overall security posture of the corporation and ensure its long-term success.

Preventing Counterfeit Goods

Counterfeit goods pose a significant threat to corporations, not only in terms of financial losses but also in terms of reputation damage. To prevent counterfeit goods from infiltrating the supply chain, it is essential for organizations to implement robust security measures. This subchapter will explore strategies for preventing counterfeit goods and protecting the integrity of the corporation's products.

One of the key steps in preventing counterfeit goods is to establish strong relationships with trusted suppliers. By thoroughly vetting suppliers and conducting regular audits, organizations can ensure that the products they are receiving are authentic. It is also important to establish clear guidelines and expectations regarding product quality and authenticity, and to communicate these requirements to suppliers effectively.

Another crucial aspect of preventing counterfeit goods is to implement effective monitoring and surveillance systems. This may include using technology such as RFID tags or serialization to track products throughout the supply chain. By closely monitoring the movement of products and identifying any anomalies or discrepancies, organizations can quickly detect and address potential counterfeit goods.

In addition to proactive measures, organizations should also be prepared to respond swiftly and decisively in the event that counterfeit goods are discovered. This may involve conducting thorough investigations, working with law enforcement agencies, and taking legal action against counterfeiters. By demonstrating a zero-tolerance approach to counterfeit goods, organizations can deter potential counterfeiters and protect their brand reputation.

Overall, preventing counterfeit goods requires a multi-faceted approach that involves collaboration across different security departments within the organization. By working together to implement robust security measures, organizations can effectively safeguard their products and maintain the trust of their customers. In the ever-evolving landscape of global commerce, it is essential for corporations to remain vigilant and proactive in their efforts to prevent counterfeit goods.

Mitigating Supplier Fraud

Supplier fraud poses a significant risk to large corporations, as dishonest suppliers can manipulate prices, deliver substandard goods or services, or engage in other unethical practices that can harm the company's reputation and bottom line. To effectively mitigate the risk of supplier fraud, corporations must implement robust controls and procedures within their Supply Chain Security Department.

One key strategy for mitigating supplier fraud is conducting thorough due diligence on potential suppliers before entering into any business relationships. This includes verifying the supplier's credentials, conducting background checks, and obtaining references from previous clients. By thoroughly vetting suppliers, corporations can identify any red flags or warning signs of potential fraudulent activity before it occurs.

Another important step in mitigating supplier fraud is implementing strong contract management practices. Contracts with suppliers should clearly outline expectations, deliverables, payment terms, and dispute resolution mechanisms. By ensuring that contracts are well-drafted and legally binding, corporations can hold suppliers accountable for any fraudulent behavior and seek legal recourse if necessary.

Regular monitoring and auditing of supplier relationships is also essential for mitigating fraud. The Supply Chain Security Department should conduct periodic reviews of supplier performance, financial stability, and compliance with contractual obligations. By proactively monitoring suppliers, corporations can detect any signs of fraudulent activity early on and take corrective action to protect their interests.

In addition to these proactive measures, corporations should also establish clear reporting mechanisms for employees to raise concerns about potential supplier fraud. Employees should be encouraged to report any suspicious behavior or irregularities they observe in supplier interactions, and whistleblower protection policies should be in place to safeguard employees who come forward with information about fraudulent activity. By fostering a culture of transparency and accountability, corporations can create a strong defense against supplier fraud and protect their reputation and financial health.

Chapter 11: Executive Protection Department

Providing Security Services for Executives

In the corporate world, executives often find themselves in high-risk situations due to their visibility and importance within the organization. As a result, it is crucial to have a dedicated Executive Protection Department to provide security services tailored to their unique needs. This department is responsible for ensuring the safety and well-being of top-level executives, including providing personal security details, secure transportation, and security assessments of their residences and travel itineraries.

The Executive Protection Department works closely with other security departments within the corporation to coordinate efforts and share information on potential threats. This collaboration is essential for creating a comprehensive security strategy that addresses all aspects of executive protection, from physical security measures to cybersecurity protocols. By working together, these departments can identify vulnerabilities and implement effective security measures to mitigate risks.

Securing the Corporate Fortress: A Guide to Managing Different Security Departments in a Large Corporation

One of the key roles of the Executive Protection Department is to conduct threat assessments for high-profile executives. These assessments involve evaluating potential threats, such as physical harm, kidnapping, or extortion, and developing strategies to mitigate these risks. By staying one step ahead of potential threats, the Executive Protection Department can proactively protect executives and prevent security incidents before they occur.

In addition to providing physical security services, the Executive Protection Department is also responsible for ensuring the privacy and confidentiality of executives' information. This includes implementing secure communication channels, protecting sensitive data, and monitoring for any potential breaches or leaks. By safeguarding executives' digital assets, the department helps to prevent cyber threats and ensure the integrity of the corporation's information.

Overall, the Executive Protection Department plays a critical role in safeguarding the well-being and reputation of high-profile executives within a large corporation. By providing tailored security services, collaborating with other security departments, conducting threat assessments, and protecting digital assets, this department helps to create a secure environment for executives to carry out their duties effectively and confidently.

Personal Security Details

Personal Security Details are a crucial aspect of ensuring the safety and security of high-profile executives within a large corporation. This subchapter will delve into the importance of providing personal security details for executives and the key considerations that need to be taken into account when managing this aspect of security.

One of the primary goals of personal security details is to protect executives from potential threats, both physical and cyber. This involves conducting thorough risk assessments to identify any vulnerabilities and developing a comprehensive security plan to mitigate these risks. It is essential for security professionals to work closely with executives to understand their specific security needs and preferences, as well as to keep them informed about any potential threats or security incidents.

Personal security details may include providing secure transportation for executives, conducting background checks on individuals who come into contact with them, and implementing access control measures to prevent unauthorized individuals from approaching them. It is also important to have a designated team of trained security personnel who are responsible for overseeing the security of executives at all times.

In addition to physical security measures, personal security details also encompass cybersecurity measures to protect executives' digital assets and personal information. This includes implementing strong password policies, encrypting communications, and monitoring for any signs of cyber threats or hacking attempts. It is crucial for security professionals to stay up-to-date on the latest cybersecurity trends and best practices to ensure the ongoing security of executives' digital assets.

Furthermore, personal security details should be integrated into the overall security strategy of the corporation, working in conjunction with other security departments such as Physical Security, Cybersecurity, and Risk Management. By collaborating with these departments, security professionals can ensure a holistic approach to security that addresses all potential threats and vulnerabilities.

Overall, personal security details play a critical role in safeguarding high-profile executives within a large corporation. By implementing comprehensive security measures, conducting regular risk assessments, and staying vigilant against potential threats, security professionals can help protect executives from harm and ensure the ongoing security of the corporation as a whole.

Secure Transportation for High-Profile Executives

In the corporate world, high-profile executives are often targets for various threats, ranging from kidnapping to corporate espionage. As such, it is crucial for organizations to have a dedicated Executive Protection Department that can provide secure transportation for these individuals. This subchapter will delve into the importance of secure transportation for high-profile executives and provide insights on how to effectively manage this aspect of executive protection.

One of the key considerations when it comes to securing transportation for high-profile executives is the level of threat they face. Executives who are involved in sensitive negotiations, high-stakes deals, or are in the public eye are more likely to be targeted by malicious actors. In such cases, it is imperative to have robust security measures in place to ensure their safety during transit.

Secure transportation for high-profile executives goes beyond simply providing them with a chauffeured vehicle. It involves conducting thorough risk assessments, implementing stringent access control measures, and deploying highly trained security personnel to accompany the executives at all times. Additionally, secure transportation protocols should be regularly reviewed and updated to adapt to changing security threats and circumstances.

In addition to physical security measures, cybersecurity also plays a critical role in ensuring the safety of high-profile executives during transit. Hackers and cybercriminals may attempt to target executives' digital devices and communications, posing a significant risk to their safety and the confidentiality of sensitive information. Therefore, it is essential for organizations to integrate cybersecurity best practices into their secure transportation protocols.

Overall, secure transportation for high-profile executives is a multifaceted endeavor that requires a comprehensive approach to security. By leveraging the expertise of the Executive Protection Department, organizations can mitigate risks, safeguard their executives, and maintain the integrity of their operations. It is imperative for security professionals to stay vigilant, proactive, and adaptable in order to effectively manage the security challenges associated with executive transportation in today's dynamic and high-risk business environment.

Chapter 12: Conclusion and Future Trends in Corporate Security Management

Recap of Managing Different Security Departments

Securing the Corporate Fortress: A Guide to Managing Different Security Departments in a Large Corporation

In this subchapter, we will recap the key points discussed in managing different security departments within a large corporation. Each department plays a crucial role in protecting the organization from various security threats and risks, and it is essential for security professionals to effectively manage and coordinate the efforts of these departments to ensure the overall security of the corporation.

The Physical Security Department is responsible for securing the physical premises of the corporation, including access control, surveillance, and security patrols. This department plays a critical role in preventing unauthorized access and protecting the organization's assets from theft and vandalism. Effective management of the Physical Security Department involves implementing robust security measures and protocols to ensure the safety of employees, visitors, and property.

The Cybersecurity Department is tasked with managing the organization's digital assets and protecting them from cyber threats, such as hacking and data breaches. With the increasing frequency and sophistication of cyber attacks, it is crucial for security professionals to stay ahead of emerging threats and implement proactive security measures to safeguard the organization's digital infrastructure. Managing the Cybersecurity Department involves staying informed about the latest cyber threats and technologies and implementing effective security strategies to mitigate risks.

The Information Security Department is responsible for ensuring the confidentiality, integrity, and availability of the corporation's information assets. This department plays a crucial role in protecting sensitive information from unauthorized access and ensuring that data is secure and accessible when needed. Effective management of the Information Security Department involves implementing robust security controls, conducting regular security audits, and providing ongoing training to employees on security best practices.

Securing the Corporate Fortress: A Guide to Managing Different Security Departments in a Large Corporation

The Risk Management Department is tasked with identifying and assessing potential security risks to the corporation and developing strategies to mitigate them. This department plays a crucial role in helping the organization anticipate and prepare for security threats, such as natural disasters, cyber attacks, and supply chain disruptions. Managing the Risk Management Department involves conducting thorough risk assessments, developing risk mitigation plans, and collaborating with other security departments to address security vulnerabilities.

In conclusion, managing different security departments within a large corporation requires a strategic and coordinated approach to ensure the overall security of the organization. By effectively managing and coordinating the efforts of departments such as Physical Security, Cybersecurity, Information Security, Risk Management, and others, security professionals can help protect the corporation from a wide range of security threats and risks. It is essential for security professionals to stay informed about emerging security trends and technologies and work collaboratively with other departments to create a strong and resilient security posture for the organization.

Emerging Trends in Corporate Security

As the landscape of corporate security continues to evolve, professionals in different security departments within large corporations must stay abreast of emerging trends to effectively manage and mitigate security risks. One such trend is the increasing convergence of physical security and cybersecurity departments. With the rise of smart buildings and Internet of Things (IoT) devices, there is a growing need for these two departments to work closely together to secure both the physical premises and digital assets of the corporation.

Another emerging trend in corporate security is the shift towards proactive threat intelligence and risk management. Instead of solely focusing on reactive security measures, risk management departments are now utilizing advanced analytics and threat intelligence to identify potential security risks before they materialize. By taking a proactive approach to security, corporations can better protect their assets and mitigate potential threats.

Securing the Corporate Fortress: A Guide to Managing Different Security Departments in a Large Corporation

The increasing reliance on cloud services and remote work has also led to a rise in the importance of information security departments. As employees access corporate data from various locations and devices, information security professionals must implement robust security measures to ensure the confidentiality, integrity, and availability of sensitive information. This trend highlights the critical role that information security departments play in safeguarding the corporation's digital assets.

Additionally, compliance departments are facing new challenges as security regulations and industry standards continue to evolve. With the introduction of regulations such as the General Data Protection Regulation (GDPR) and the California Consumer Privacy Act (CCPA), compliance professionals must stay up-to-date on the latest requirements to ensure that the corporation remains in compliance. Failure to comply with these regulations can result in significant financial penalties and reputational damage for the corporation.

Overall, the field of corporate security is constantly evolving, and professionals in different security departments must adapt to these emerging trends to effectively manage security risks within a large corporation. By staying informed, collaborating across departments, and implementing proactive security measures, security professionals can help secure the corporate fortress and protect the organization from potential threats.

Recommendations for Improving Corporate Security Practices

In today's increasingly digital and interconnected world, corporate security practices are more important than ever. To ensure the safety and protection of a large corporation's assets, employees, and reputation, it is crucial for security departments to continuously evaluate and improve their practices. This subchapter will provide recommendations for enhancing corporate security practices across various departments, including Physical Security, Cybersecurity, Information Security, Risk Management, Compliance, Fraud Prevention, Emergency Response, Employee Security Awareness, Supply Chain Security, and Executive Protection.

Securing the Corporate Fortress: A Guide to Managing Different Security Departments in a Large Corporation

First and foremost, it is essential for all security departments within a large corporation to collaborate and communicate effectively. By working together, sharing information, and coordinating efforts, security teams can better identify and address potential vulnerabilities and threats. Regular meetings, joint training sessions, and cross-departmental exercises can help foster a culture of cooperation and unity among different security departments.

Secondly, investing in cutting-edge technology and tools is key to improving corporate security practices. From advanced access control systems and surveillance cameras to sophisticated cybersecurity software and encryption technologies, leveraging the latest security solutions can help enhance the overall security posture of the organization. Regularly updating and upgrading security systems, conducting vulnerability assessments, and staying informed about emerging threats and trends in the security landscape are also essential steps to take.

Moreover, developing comprehensive security policies and procedures tailored to the specific needs and risks of the organization is crucial. Each security department should have well-defined roles, responsibilities, and protocols in place to respond to security incidents effectively. Regularly reviewing and updating security policies, conducting security awareness training for employees, and performing regular audits and assessments can help ensure that security practices remain robust and effective.

Additionally, establishing strong relationships with external partners, such as law enforcement agencies, industry associations, and security consultants, can provide valuable resources and expertise to support corporate security efforts. Collaborating with external experts can help security departments stay informed about emerging threats, best practices, and regulatory requirements, as well as access specialized skills and technologies that may not be available in-house.

Securing the Corporate Fortress: A Guide to Managing Different Security Departments in a Large Corporation

Lastly, promoting a culture of security awareness and vigilance among employees is critical to enhancing corporate security practices. Security departments should prioritize educating and training employees on security best practices, raising awareness about common threats and scams, and encouraging reporting of suspicious activities. By fostering a security-conscious culture within the organization, employees can become active participants in protecting the company's assets and data from security risks and threats.

www.ingramcontent.com/pod-product-compliance
Lightning Source LLC
Chambersburg PA
CBHW082241220526
45479CB00005B/1299